Resilient

Resilient

A Year of Soul-Searching through Poetry

Nathaniel Sanderson

RESOURCE *Publications* • Eugene, Oregon

RESILIENT
A Year of Soul-Searching through Poetry

Resource Publications
An Imprint of Wipf and Stock Publishers
199 W. 8th Ave., Suite 3
Eugene, OR 97401

www.wipfandstock.com

PAPERBACK ISBN: 978-1-7252-8661-0
HARDCOVER ISBN: 978-1-7252-8662-7
EBOOK ISBN: 978-1-7252-8663-4

11/17/20

For Matt and Alina,
without whom I would still be lost to my anger.

Contents

Contents

Contents

Preface

2018 was a tough year. It started with several hospital visits and specialists telling me that I was very near dying, but none of them quite knowing what to do about it. With that in the background, I had attempted to pursue my own business, the stress of which was overwhelming. Slowly, but steadily, I fell into a depressive spiral and at the end of the year, I attempted to take my own life. I lived, clearly, and I wanted to get back on the horse. I found poetry as a refuge through all the darkness and the mess. Poetry saved my life, and I am hoping to share it with the world.

I figured I would open with the poem I wrote about my suicide attempt, even though I wrote it months after my attempt, so be ready for that. The book chronicles my journey through the ups and downs of 2019. I began the year as a house painter scraping the poverty line and will end it as a therapist helping people with ADHD and ASD/Aspergers through the mess that we call life. When I started the year, I was angry and hopeless, but now I have hope and think the world deserves a piece of that hope.

From my attempt, I move on to the new year and my struggles with still being alive, despite all that had happened. As the year progressed, the fires of my anger began to smolder and die. For a while, it was replaced by hopelessness, until a sense of purpose filled me. Anger makes the occasional return, but loneliness started to really get loud, as did my self-doubt. I battled with my loneliness for a long while, trying desperately to feel that I was worth living for, and that life had meaning outside of having a partner.

Then, as the summer began, I started training for a new job. I had no formal education for the job, but my bosses saw the skills I'd acquired over years of youth work and knew I could handle it. That didn't stop me from feeling like an imposter. Still, I rose up to the challenge and did not give in. I would not be denied my destiny. So I fought on.

Now, months into the job, I feel like I've earned a place at the Center. I no longer feel out of place as I walk into my office. I no longer wake up hating myself. I still worry about seeing my depression, but I've learned how to talk to it in a way that is healthy for me. Hopefully these poems can help other people as they face a similar journey.

Rebirth

"Worthless,
Your life is forfeit.
You can't even keep up your fitness.
There is no one who sees you as fit.
Why does it matter?
You couldn't be fatter!
If you sit in a chair it'll shatter!
And your friends are worse for your help!
You think you could ever be worthy?
You're so big you can't be sturdy,
As your company drowns in the kelp!"
The voice shouted loudly,
As I sit in the seat of my Civic.
"Engine's running, might as well end it."
I reached for the shifter,
I pressed the clutch,
Ready to end this drifter.
Then Clarity slapped me across the face.
I hadn't realized I'd lost that much.
I turned off the car,
And went for a walk to give myself space.
I'd been a hairsbreadth from going too far.
I looked up, grateful for the stars.
A half hour and a coffee later,
I felt brave enough to look at the place I'd almost ended my life.

I felt a little safer,
Free for a moment from the strife.

Defiance

Defiance fills my veins
It courses through my blood.
I feel it as an anticipation,
It soaks me like the rain,
It remains like a stain.
It carries me like a flood.
My destiny is forward,
I will not be denied.
My destiny is onward,
I will not hide.

The Burden of Purpose

I am burdened with great purpose,
I will cast off the yoke of my darkness.
Strength, I will gather in surplus.
Today I rise, defined in starkness.
There are none who can stand before me,
I will not be denied my destiny.
The negativity rises all around,
Lying in the low places I cannot see,
Gathering the strength to surround.
In those I trust and love abound,
When I was falling it surged forth,
Pouring out of my support net.
Surging from East, West, South, and North.
My former weakness they sought, I bet.
Little did they know,
The power that I have in stow.

I Will Face My Destiny

I'll be honest, destiny is odd.
Once I believed I'd rise above kings,
Yet now I sit in the sod.
Once I thought I'd fly on eagle's wings,
Yet now I live in the dirt.
But this is not the end of my story.
Mental illness be damned, I will rise.
This is but the beginning of my fury.
Judgement be damned, the earth will hear my cries.
From the ashes of defeat I come,
Woe to those who would stand in my way.
From the worries of an old life, I'm numb.
Woe to those who would have me stay.
It is with death and destiny that I flirt.

Worries Will Not Hold Me Down

My worries; fetters that held me fast,
Linked to the wall by the chains of the past.
Unable to think, afraid I'd breathed my last,
I sat, hurt and done, always aghast.
Until I realized that the stone was mine to cast.
I broke the chains, my enemies I would outlast,
I shattered my fetters with quite the blast.
Free at last from my worries and woes,
I will stand triumphant over my foes.

Frostbite

It was cold at first,
And I pushed.
Freeing my car, I felt cursed,
I was bushed.
The cold faded as I toiled,
But then fire came.
Yet still I refused to be foiled,
The frost said, "Same!"
But at last I was free,
So I left.
The frost laughed with glee,
I was bereft.
That's when I began to shake,
The frost won.
My feet, fire tried to take.
I barely made it to my house,
But I did, so now I can grouse.

The Villain

Many dreams broke there,
On the anvil of your ambition.
Crafted into your lair,
Taking life, love, labor, and tuition.
To bring your empire to fruition.
My dreams you took and you buried,
And used my labor to lay the foundation.
My love you took and you hurried,
Building the community of submission,
For your empire of superstition.
No longer will I lie in the mass grave,
Filled with the bones of your last creation.
My life, now a road will pave,
A road to your destruction.

I Will Rise

I will rise up,
Not for the loss of my enemies.
I will drink this cup,
To stand and rise out of the fleas.
Today I shall rise,
The shining sun on my back,
No longer will I fear their spies,
There will be nothing that I lack.
This rage that sits in my breast,
Will guide me through the night.
As the curtains of blackness will attest,
I will be feared for I am bright!
The gloom will run from my path,
And all those who stand before me,
Will face my wrath.

Pleasant Anger

"Patience," I whisper to my rage,
As he rears against the reins.
"First we must set the stage,
And then you can fill my veins."
"I would rather not suffer them,"
Rage responds, horking phlegm.
"Our victory will be more complete,
Should we pursue justice,"
I say, regarding a sea of concrete.
"We need proper fuel for your fire to reach the precipice."
"Yes, yes, I quite like this plan,"
Rage says, smiling like a mad man.
Our eyes meet, mine a sea and his aflame,
"Together we will win this all the same."

Victory

The arrogance of you,
To stand here and be nice.
While I suffered out on the ice,
You spat on me from the shore.
You played the victim once more,
Made me look like the villain.
I hurt while you were chillin'.
I suffered while you partied.
I stared Death in the face and almost died,
And I would have welcomed his embrace!
But no, Clarity came too,
And she's a beauty, that Clarity.
She pulled me right back to reality.
I said farewell to Death,
I returned to the race.
I took my first breath,
My first breath free of you.

The Backstabber

You stand before me,
Offering your hand.
Friends, once, were we,
You changed that when you made your stand.
No longer can I walk the land,
You left me dying on the strand.
Yet you dare ask, you flea.
You dare ask me to take you back,
To ignore the scars that cover my back,
To put pain in a sack,
When forgiveness is a skill you lack!
You poisoned the band,
Such that denying you earned me such flack.
You may think the cost too great,
Well, woe to you mate,
I'll pay the cost with no debate.

The Forest

A gentle rumble fills the air,
As I walk the forest fair.
Birds join the chorus with their flair,
Crying out loudly without a care.
Splashes of color abound as they fly,
Complementing the flowers where they lie.
The cedars bring their needles to bear,
As a river winds gently by.
I break the clearing and find a stair,
Clinging to the cliffs by a hair.
Vines surround the stone and break it free,
At the top a terrace and a chair,
It stands overlooking the great sea.

The Mountain

How do you climb a mountain?
It's immense and daunting,
And my strength isn't like a fountain!
Yet there are people who do it without balking.
I've heard it starts with one step,
Followed closely by a hand reaching.
And you repeat the process with pep.
But I'm tired and I feel weak.
It's not that I fear being too meek,
It's that I'm too tired to find the strength I seek.
I'm not worried that this bucket will leak,
Just that it doesn't hold enough water.
But maybe the old saying is right,
That a mountain does begin with a single step,
And maybe I don't need the strength to add that pep.

Rising Again

I will stand tall.
I will rise once more,
Even though I had quite the fall.
My spirit is weary and sore, but still burns at the core.
The mountains will hear my roar!
As I stand before those that would hurt me,
I will give no ground.
They will feel the sound,
The sound of one once bound.
Now I am free!
I will not pay their fee,
I will not lie with the fleas.
So, I will stand.
Even though everything tells me no,
I will claim this land.
I will measure up to what's in stow.

Fury 1

I am the Fury in the Night!
I am not going to take flight,
I will stand and be bright.
The darkness will feel fright,
And I will no longer wait.
The path before me is narrow and straight,
And I'll run this race.
I will set the pace,
My enemies will know by sight,
That I have returned to this place.

Fury 2

I am the Fury in the Night,
The fire that burns bright.
The storm that taught the Darkness fright!
The indomitable knight, in rusted armor,
Who rose from the dusty earth,
With wrath in his eyes,
Carrying his destiny with ardor.
I gave hope a new birth,
And now I look to the skies,
And I know that the Darkness has no spies.
I am equal to this life,
And I will survive this strife.

Fury 3

I am the Fury in the Night, I survived the blight.
Now I have a life to rebuild,
Where once I grasped at straws.
The hole in my heart that self-love filled,
Was put there by those with no cause.
They didn't even pause,
But I rose from those ashes,
And I'm filled with a hope that no one dashes.
My future is bright,
Because I will use this damned fright,
Because I will not back down from this fight,
Because I can't give up,
And I refuse to drink the poisoned cup,
That the Darkness offered when it had me to sup.
That would have been quite the hiccup.
No longer would the Fury in the Night burn,
No longer would the Darkness fear,
No longer would those with that selfsame hole in their heart find solace!
So I remain stern,
And I will take this life that is mine to steer,
And drive it into the morning.
For in the morning you find those that you would miss,
Who are lost to their own mess,
And in need of love.
Love that I can bring,
Love that would be missed had I drank that cup.

Who Are You?

Who are you?
I'm not asking for your name.
I'm asking for the inner beast,
The one that you seek to tame.
You know the one.
The beast that fears nothing,
The beast that does the fighting.
The beast with its mouth frothing,
That backs you up in the night.
So, who are you?
Are you a flame that burns bright?
Or perhaps a hunter that stays out of sight?
Who do you reach for,
When the enemy is at your door?
When everything is sore,
When you tire of this war,
What comes out of that cave?
I'll tell you mine to help you find yours.
On a normal day I am meek,
Barely able to operate this ship's oars.
Yet when the night has sought to find me weak,
Out comes the Fury in the Night,
My rage is full and bright,
Carrying me onward like a knight.
Sword pitted and rusting,
But drawn nonetheless.

Armor damaged and breaking,
But donned nonetheless.
Thus, my enemies know fear.

The Runner

It was getting dark as he ran.
The chill of the evening setting in.
The absurdity of his grand plan,
Resting ever on the horizon.
He ran nonetheless,
Each footfall loudly proclaiming the next.
The fire in his limbs fought the cold,
As his resolve made him bold,
He would reach his goal as he foretold.
On anything less he would not be sold.

Lonely

It's subtle as it seeps into my bones,
Slow and sneaking in the shadows.
It reminds me of dying meadows,
As it seeks to break my foundation stones.
The loneliness tells me I am but one half.
And while I know the lie in its words,
I can't help but feel like I'm missing a member of staff.
I long for someone to help me tend the herds.
My heart aches for another,
But I fear the pain of the other,
And I worry that I might smother.
I'm on my knees in this pain.
But perhaps that is the point,
To open my heart and be hurt.
For without vulnerability there can be no joint,
And without openness there's no need to flirt.
So perhaps I should rise,
And stand before their spies.
Chase this loneliness to the skies,
And take a dive into unknown sties.
I deserve to be loved,
So curse this loneliness,
And curse this fear.
I will share my beautiful mess,
And I will find someone dear,
Because I am worth the effort.

Ilyn 1

Long have I suffered in the dark,
Beaten and bruised and left in the cold.
Today I finally walk free in the park,
Life may yet let me be bold.
Now to get this life in order,
And heal this mess on my shoulder.
I will protect this land,
By Fury's side I'll stand.

Will This Misery Ever End?

What is the fucking point?
It seems that for every fucking victory,
There's just another monster in the joint!
When will I be free of this misery?
When will this just fucking end,
And let me be a normal person again?

What Will Make Me Whole?

Rage burns in my soul.
My heart's a fire, and I'm adding coal,
Is it wrong that this makes me whole?
But it's starting to take its toll.
I feel weak,
Maybe I'm just meek,
Maybe I'll find the peace I seek,
If I just break that freak!
Is it wrong that these thoughts make me whole?
But they're starting to take their toll.
The loneliness is seeping in.
I'm succumbing to this sin.
There's nothing left in my bin.
Do I even deserve to be whole?
I don't think I can afford this toll.
I should just leave it all behind,
Leave people with nothing to find.
I think that would be kind.
I don't deserve to be whole,
I was never worthy enough for this toll.
Unless I am.
And these feelings are a scam,
Lies from my past; a sham.
I'm already whole!
Feelings are a guide and not a toll!

Today, I will face the rising tide,
I will stand, even with no one by my side.
In death, I will no longer confide.
I will help make this world whole,
For that is my toll.
To be a guide to those still lost,
To help those who can't afford the cost,
To warm those out in the frost.
Love will make me whole.
Love can cover any toll.

Peace

How does one live in the calm land of peace?
I was bred for conflict long before I was born.
My ancestors are conquerors from Iceland to Greece.
I am burly, stocky, and move like an oncoming storm.
My visage strikes fear into the hearts of the innocent,
While the land around me thrives and reeks of mint.
My heart races and never pauses, not even for a stint.
I feel like steel looking at the world like flint,
Ready to burn the kindling.

Fear

Fear robs me of my resolve.
It makes me shake.
It tells me I'm a fake,
And I can't help but believe.
These thoughts do not relieve,
They steal my will to go on,
And I can't even breathe.
I need to shake this feeling,
Before it breaks through the ceiling,
And takes me on a rampage away from everything I love.

Regret

This pain seeps into my soul,
You, my only regret.
I got lost on the shoal,
And now I always seem to fret.

I was lost,
Consumed by the frost.
Those who claimed to love us,
Were the loudest in the chorus,
The chorus of lies about you.

This pain burdens my soul,
And you're my only regret.
I was manipulated like a fool,
And my regrets make me fret.

My heart aches,
Seeing you gave me the shakes.
There's so much I wanted to say,
When I saw you today,
But the pain was overwhelming.

I see the pain in your soul,
And it fuels my regret.
I burned you like a coal,
Your eyes tell me how you fret.

Why did I have to hurt you?
You, who was always so kind.
Oh why, why did I ever leave?
And why did I burn you as I left?

I long to mend your soul,
And not just to ease my regret,
But to make us both whole,
And to take away your frets.

Lonely 2

As ever, I stare into the precipice,
Where so many live in harmony.
Yet, I am barred access.
I accidentally force the issue eagerly,
And end up scaring off potential partners.
I feel like a failure again,
Overwhelmed and stuck in a den.
Perhaps it's for the best that I'm lost in the firs.

Lost

My life feels directionless,
Without cause.
With nothing but this mess,
I take pause.
See these flaws?
I wish I was stronger,
That I could run longer,
That I didn't feel so empty.
I look in the mirror and see a broken man.
A flea.
Where's the plan?
Where do I even begin?
How do I get free from this din,
And see the light of day again?
I've pondered this in moments of zen.
And in the strife,
All I know is that I have this life.
This one chance to make a difference.
This one time to matter,
Maybe I just need to change the cadence.
To set goals and get at 'er.

I need to rise from this muck,
Rise before I get stuck,
And stop feeling down on my luck,
And actually start to make a plan for my future self.
I will hop off this shelf,
And begin to change the world.

Why?

Why?
After all I've done.
After all I've suffered.
Am I just the cursed son?
A moldy cheese curd?
I've fought so damn hard,
I've held nothing back,
And yet I still get the sack,
I still hand the officer my card.
I am done with this disorganized mess.
I will suffer nothing less,
Than a semblance of order.
I can't keep losing due to past failings.
I'll be on top of all my things,
And finally find peace in this life.

The End

You will look your end in the eye.
This is the guarantee of life.
Today I urge you to rise and tell that end you won't die.
Tell it that you'll survive this strife!

Fury 4

Please do not think that every breath I take is not in defiance of this cruel and listless world we live in.

I refuse to be broke again.

I refuse to give up.

I am the Fury in the Night, and my shouts will be heard.

Take Your Stand

As the night draws to a close on this era,
There was a man who dared stand before a few hundred youth.
He spoke not of fixing this world uncouth,
But of taking a stand in your own strata.
He used this amazing metaphor,
Of a young man on a beach.
He hadn't set out to change the world,
But to give just one mere starfish the chance to stand tall and reach.

Entering the Gates

I stand before the gates.
Behind me stand the once-burning ruins.
I fear what lies in this city I have my shoe in,
But there is naught behind me but hate.
The city is enticing,
It promises love and healing.
But I am so used to the burning,
And now I fear the future.
It looks bright and promising,
But my mind is waiting for this image to fracture,
And reveal once more the beast within.

Let Us Fight

The time has come.
It's time we followed our intuition,
And create an institution,
Of inquisition.
To make an incision,
In corporate inflation.
To challenge their station,
And rise like the Haitians,
Casting off the bonds of submission,
From corporate nations.

Engaging with Apathy

This apathy, it is overwhelming.
A feeling of not actually feeling,
And me, teeming with the fucker.
I wish I was angry,
Because at least it would have meaning!
Instead I just feel like a sucker,
Flatlining feelings with no glee.
It's just so damn stupid,
But I can't build enough emotion to make this fluid.
I'd love to say that I'm frustrated,
But I'm not even overrated.
I just want to shout my sadness to the sailing winds and ignite some
salient passion in my veins to solve this miserable salt that saps the
life from my sapience.
I want my brain back.
This flat line will hit the sack.
I will take up the attack,
And grab Rage off the rack,
And win this war!
You think yourself subtle?
I will find the root of this apathetic mind,
And give chase until its core I find.
Is it the pain?
Is it the lack of gym?

Huh?
Answer me, you slag!
Know that I will find you.
"Do you matter?
You paint walls, don't flatter.
Your life has done nothing!
Where is your impact?
You think anyone is thriving?
I know your resolve is cracked.
Ha! You think yourself a god?
We both know you belong in the sod."
I am the Fury in the Night,
I've climbed out of worse scraps than this,
And I've already won this game of chess.
You have no leg to stand on.
I've built communities from here to the horizon.
Give me my feelings back, you slag!
You hold no power here, you hag!
This is my home,
It is not for you to hold the stone.
I've changed more lives than you could comprehend,
Even in painting walls I've got love to send.
And while I'm not a god,
I belong firmly above the sod.
Loving myself is healthy,
So stop holding me to these unhealthy standards.
I have one last thing to say to thee,
Pay attention, as I know you're haggard.
I matter.

Did I stutter?
Perhaps I don't flatter,
And maybe I got a little fatter,
But I matter.
So don't you dare blather!

The Block

As I delve deeper into myself,
It looms on the horizon.
Once again, I grab a book from this shelf,
Once again, I find no words thereon.
This looming force is exhausting;
A physical barrier I cannot breach.
It sits with a toll it's exacting,
And I know my freedom lies just beyond reach!
What is this mess?
Is there a way through?
This door I've found feels like a jest,
It says the key lies in confronting him,
You know who.
The one who left me dead for a hymn.

I Won't Back Down

Real life is a cruel mistress.
It strikes at the worst possible moment,
Right when you're starting to drown in your own mess.
I just want to run away and pitch a tent.
But I won't.
I will rise higher when life yells, 'Don't!"
I will not suffer to live in this defeat.
I will rise once again to my feet.
I know I'll get knocked down again,
But I am whole and refuse to live back in that den!
I will avoid the surrounding fen,
And take good care of myself.

10K

Today I stand as a champion.
Months ago, I planned this moment.
Now I finally get to hear the bell's clarion.
As I stand resolute on this monument,
I have conquered this goal.
I stare out at the old shoal,
That cursed placed where once I was in jail.
Now I am free.
I have set my sail,
And go forth to achieve my destiny.

The Brink of Death

I've come from the brink of death,
And trust me, it was a close thing.
I almost breathed my last breath,
And now I stand here among the living.
So I'll make something of this new life,
I'll live it to the fullest.
I'll bring love, life, laughter in the face of strife,
So as many as possible don't die to that selfsame mess.

Victory is Near

I stand so close to victory.
Every step forward is hard won and messy.
I've been on this journey for so long,
And all I have to show for it are lessons learned.
But lessons are better than some shiny gong,
And feel much more earned.
So, I'll keep on moving,
Though my thighs shake and quiver.
And I'll keep on improving,
Though the night makes me shake and shiver.

And now, standing in triumph so clear,
Rising up and helping those far and near,
My life at last has meaning.
And I awake in the morning with glee,
In this purpose-filled life I'm keening,
The darkness has packed its bag and begun to flee!

2k

The road rushes by beneath my feet,
My own body is the opponent I wish to beat.
Breathe in. Left foot. Right foot. Left foot.
My resolve is a fire in which my faith is put.
Pain blossoms in my right lung,
My body screams at me for flapping my tongue.
Breathe out. Right foot. Left foot. Right foot.
My muscles, like a phoenix, rise from the soot.
Halfway there and the pain finally melts away,
Although the fire in my lungs chooses to stay.
Breathe in. Left foot. Right foot. Left foot.
I've passed the threshold and my weakness is caput!
Endorphins scream triumph in my veins,
As my running partner battles me for the lanes.
Breathe out. Right foot. Left foot. Right foot.
My strength is finally afoot,
And my vigor renews as the end comes in sight,
So I sprint for the end with a hero's might!
Breathe in. I stumble.
Breathe out. I grab water.
Breathe in. My running partner and I mumble.
Breathe out. I lean on him like an otter.
Breathe in. Left foot. Right foot. Left foot.
I have no more energy to input.
Breathe out. Right foot. Left foot. Right foot.
So I just let my thoughts output.

Imposter

I feel like such an imposter.
I don't feel like I've earned this,
And these feelings in my heart are like kids I foster.
I should run away and crawl into the abyss.
That wretched voice has returned.
"You stand where others belong,"
It whispers as though it was spurned.
Who am I to say it's wrong?
You know, I even hit an old low,
It has felled me with one mighty blow.
I know that I should get up,
And rise to the occasion,
But the voice just won't let up.
Reginald, I name you.
I'll get past your evasion,
And I'll get up too.
I've lived my life in fear of your might,
Reginald, the deceiver.
Reginald, who once shone bright.
Reginald, keeper of confidence.
You echo words of my past life like a broken receiver,
And I know that that is no coincidence.
Yet still, you are the source of my fright.
I've brought you low before,
But perhaps all you need is cold logic.
So here's some knowledge to make you soar.

All my life I've worked towards this moment.
Every scrap of volunteering,
Every late-night conversation by some monument,
Every youth I helped in steering.
All of it.
All of it led me here.
I have this skillset,
And the last thing holding me back is fear.
Trust me, this will be good for us.
We are built for this, I bet.
So, for tonight, let me be Horus,
And we can debrief afterwards.
Reginald, the intellectual.
Let us move forward,
And gather something nice and factual.
"Tonight, we shall speak,
But know that I am not meek.
Gather the data you seek,
And fear, I shall not leak.
Full access you shall be granted,
As I sit in judgement like a mantid."
Our destiny is forward,
We will not be denied.
Our destiny is onward,
We will not hide.

Insurance Forms

Why in Hell?
That's the fucking question.
I rang the bell,
And they tossed me some papers.
"Resume required, not a suggestion."
Why does an insurance company need a resume?
I'm not going on a god damned caper,
I'm just helping those in dismay.
But maybe they need to be sure,
That no fools, they insure.
But that wasn't in the brochure!
One final fucking hurdle.
I can jump it.
I'll not let this opportunity curdle,,
I'll do it well and call it caput.

The Debrief

We have found our destiny,
And it is indeed forward.
I thought we should hide, and I won't deny,
But that changes not that it is onward.
Hope is my horizon,
And there I shall thrive.
This life I've set my eyes on,
Helps me feel, once more, like part of the hive.

Death's Fear

I would tell you that I'm a great warrior,
The likes of which could impress mighty Horus.
The truth is though, that I've never even fought on a bus.
But trust me, I'm known by the Soul Carrier,
He who tills the dead across the river Styx.
I've stared into those lifeless sockets,
And he felt fear added to his emotional mix!
For I said, "Not today," and put my hands in my pockets.
So, am I a great fighter?
Maybe not.
But Death knows me to be brighter.
Death knows me to be wrought;
Wrought in iron,
And forged in fire,
And filled with ire.
For I've delayed our meeting twice,
And he knows that I'm not just on ice,
But that I've got quite the spine,
And intend to use it to aid others on this journey,
And look at this life that is mine,
And keep as many as possible off the gurney.
Now I will ask you,
What will you do with your journey?

The Lonely Port Master

I would say that, by and large,
I've got my emotions in healthy order.
But like a port master trying to hide an overstuffed barge,
Someone inevitably becomes a border.
Were I to speak plainly,
I'd say that I'm just so damn lonely,
And it is into that loneliness that you stumbled.
Life-loving smiles and an open ear,
That allowed my loneliness' sails to be unfurled,
But I avoid this ship and don't know how to steer.
An old and discarded companion,
My loneliness lives away from even me.
It chews at the layers of my soul's onion,
Seeping deeper and deeper into my destiny.
Years I've spent feeling lost and alone,
While friends and family miss the tone,
That cries out for intimacy.
I'll be able to keep moving,
But I'll never not be lonely, you see??
Moving from lady to lady, seeking any love?
What if I bear it proudly?
And stop pretending that I'm at peace like a dove?
Maybe I should live loudly,
Knowing that I'll experience pain,
But no longer ashamed of it like a stain.
Is that as bad as this hungered roving?

The More I Steep, the More Bitter I Become

I remember life as a young man,
Vast reserves of energy brimmed within.
None of this waking in a dull din.
Even tired, I never felt exhausted to this span.
While entire pathways in my brain are blocked,
I am even struggling to run.
Where went all that energy I had stocked?
Did I get hit by a phaser set to stun?
I remember always being able to push,
But now all my muscles are just mush.

An Open Heart

My heart aches again,
The old, familiar wound opened wide.
This time it seems I'm just too old then,
Fate, once again, is not on my side.
I sat in this ache for once,
No running, just feeling.
My heart isn't even mince,
Its layers are merely peeling.
I'm actually enjoying this acute pain,
Weird as that may sound.
It's nice to finally be able to enjoy the rain,
Instead of feeling locked in a cage like a dog in a pound.

The Path to Healing

The path to health;
What a glorious path it is.
It takes many pains out of stealth,
And sends them places I won't miss.
It meanders through a massive and lush field,
Where flowers flare and show their style.
A place where you can lay down your shield,
And not worry about needing guile.
A path to new life;
A life free of strife.

I Woke Up Angry

I'm angry and I don't know why,
But everything is setting me off.
This god damned group pulls me away from the guys,
And drags me up to the loft.
Like, what the actual fuck?
It has to be on a Thursday?
I feel helpless like a sitting duck,
All because what is under attack is my Nat Day!
And sure, "Calm down," they'll say,
But I've had enough fucking sacrifice!
Every time it's something else I love on ice,
And no compromise will suffice!
I'm unhappy.
I'm trapped.
I feel like an animal in a cage.
All I want is out of this cage, so crappy,
And back to a place where I feel happy.
I want to guard my Nat Day,
But that doesn't feel quite so sage.
And sure,
There's probably a solution out there.
But I've fallen before for this lure,
And I'd rather not lose any more hair.
It always starts with surrendering the small stuff,
Until eventually I don't have enough.

I feel like I need a guarantee,

That if I surrender here,

I won't have to keep surrendering my safety,

And I won't, for my remaining things, need to fear.

An Autumnal Wander

I wander down a lonely path,
Leaves crunching under every footfall.
The bridge I cross stands resolute against time's wrath,
Mortared stones firm through it all.
Vicious hues of orange and red vie for attention,
As a cold breeze wafts through the air.
The birds have begun their winter migration,
Leaving silence enough to share.
Peace settles into my bones,
As I sit by the river's edge.
Life seems so simple on these stones,
As though the earth's fate weren't teetering on a ledge.

Dear Old People

So what if I'm not perfect?
You think you're some kind of paragon?
Nah man, you're just another in a judgmental sect,
Content to sit around and mow your lawn.
Remember this:
I'll walk these plains long after you've died.
Everything you miss,
I'll be sure to imbibe until it's fully dried.
I'll build this temple brick by bloody brick,
Even with you trying to tear it down.
You and your ilk make me sick,
And I'll live a life that makes you frown.
I will bring love to this world with reckless abandon,
In the ways you lie about as you sing at your church luncheon!

Mark my words:
I am free from your chains.
As I walk in the cool rains,
I feel at one with humanity's herds.
But do not fret little birds,
For you haven't left my brain.
I'll even help you catch the train.
You know, the train that'll tear you in thirds,
And leave you spread across three states.

So keep spouting your hateful religion,
And decrying social rebates,
And taking from those who barely even have a smidgen.
History will forget you and not the tiny pigeon.
And when you finally meet your creator,
you'll discover that you are the only thing he hates.

Humility's Stranger

Who could rise up to me?
I don't mean to sound arrogant,
But I just feel so powerful and free.
And sure, you might say, "Hold on a moment."
But today has been a good day.
I faced a challenge I was told would be tough,
And I made it to the end without hitting the rough.
So, what do you want me to say?
Should I be more humble?
Belittle my achievements to make you feel better?
Make you happy that I'm not proud that I didn't stumble?
Why should I bear your fetter?
I worked damn hard to be here!
I broke through everything I fear,
And stared Death in his lidless eyes.
So no,
I refuse to be shy.
This is for more than just show!
I have helped people in danger,
In a way that was challenging.
So I will be humility's stranger,
I'll self-flagellate no more because I'm changing.
So you can have your self-hate,
But I'll stay here and celebrate.

Reflection

So, we're here now,
All talk of the future gone,
Bleeding into a present bow.
Peace now sprouts from my lawn,
Where once chaos reigned.
A gentle gardener I now get to be.
Hands, no more, by blood will be stained.
Such a calm land I now get to oversee.
I think we've made something of this life,
Something that can actually stand against the strife.

A Long Time Coming

Hello loneliness, my old friend.
I'd ask how you are,
But I get the messages you send.
I know I don't let them get far,
And that's because I'm afraid.
I think it's high time we talked,
Maybe Saturday if you aren't too dismayed?
I know, that time and again, I've balked,
But perhaps this time can be different.
You are big and strong and fierce,
I'm small like pocket lint.
So instead of allowing this hatchet to pierce,
Let us bury it and talk on the aftermorrow.
I promise that we will speak of your sorrow.

The Search Continues

So, I'm sure you know who I am,
But for posterity's sake, I'll give you my resume.
Around me, Death feels like a clam,
And his fear of me is great, if I may.
It is I who terrorizes the night,
It has nothing bumping in it as I walk by.
Yet my presence is gentle and bright,
A presence in which many feel no need to be shy.
I've so often been described as gregarious,
But only recently I've begun to be serious.
And no, I'm not delirious,
I'm just so damn curious.
And I want to be heard.
Because isn't that what this experience is about?
To be seen and actually feel it?
To be heard and not doubt it?
I say these things and people look at me like a zit,
Equal parts disgust and a need to assist.
Disgust at how I could be so weak.
But who hasn't gotten home, seen a zit, and been pissed?
So those layers start to melt away,
As that need for connection comes to stay,
And many souls find their rest.
So I continue to search for someone to share my mess,
And perhaps, for me, it is best,
That it has taken this long and no less.

Did I Lose My Poetry?

I find myself lost and alone.
Not that I'm lonely either,
Just that my soul lacks a tone.
I don't want my poetry to wither.
There's a fog like a loud moan,
And it chokes me like a tether.
I just can't seem to escape this fug.
How I wish to be free.
Moments ago I was so smug,
And my brain was quite lively.
Now it's just an empty mug.
What I did I do to lose my poetry?

Let's Go to Therapy

What a day we've had!
I feel like we need some therapy.
It's not like I'm not glad,
It's just that things feel a little crappy.
Perhaps all I need is a checkup,
But I know I need something.
Certainly I've had depression to sup,
But I'm not sure if he's still here lounging.

Let's Change the World

The man I once was is no more.
I would not yet recognize who I've become.
Not that I've changed at the core,
But my life is something far more handsome.
I've achieved all the goals I've set,
Less those to do with fitness.
So I need to make some new ones I bet,
And hit the gym for me to witness.
There seems to be nothing I cannot achieve,
Given time and willpower too.
Time is something I have in abundance,
And willpower happens to be my favorite tool.
In light of my soul's newfound sustenance,
To not make more goals would make me a fool.
I suppose I should just make them, right?
A day I'll plan to make my future bright.
This world will change because of me,
Even if it is one soul at a time.
Keep your eyes open so you can see,
A world changed because I chose to change mine.

Dust and Rust

Despite how good the going gets,
There is always a setback.
Something always comes calling in debts,
Telling me there's something I lack.
Once again, I rise from the dust.
Once again, I clean off this rust.
Same story every god damned time,
And yet I get back up again.
I don't know where I get the energy to rhyme,
As I stand among defeated men.
So once again I rise up from the dust,
And once again I clean this damned rust.
At some point I gotta ask why?
Why am I here? Why am I fighting?
It's not as though my endeavors are shy,
And finally it's something good that I'm sighting.
But still I'm down in the dust,
And all over my armor is that rust.
So here we go.
This time it's not for show.
I'll garden with this hoe,
And my soul will begin to glow!
An ally, I'll make of the dust,
Color and character I'll garner from the rust!
And perhaps my situation isn't all dust,
And perhaps I don't need to be so picky about this rust.

The Next Challenge

This is it team; today we challenge the next level.
I know it sounds dramatic, but I like fads.
My life has stopped swinging in a bevel.
It actually calmed down.
I found my groove,
And made a life that doesn't make me frown.
I think you would approve.
So, what is the challenge of which I speak?
Well, to be honest, I don't actually know.
I've reached this fantastic peak,
And have an abundance that's ready to sow.
So I suppose the challenge is in figuring it out.
The thing is, I don't exactly know how.
I thought I knew what it was all about,
But I think I want to have done more before life's final bow.
It's not that I don't have a life that's worth living,
I just feel that I could be doing something more.
And it's not like my life isn't giving,
It's just that I feel like I have lots more in store.
I've laid out new goals,
But I think I want to aim for something a little bigger,
Something that sets alight my soul's coals,
Something that maybe I didn't figure.
Now, what that something is, is a mystery,
But I think that that is part of the fun.

So, for now I'll enjoy the symmetry,
And plan once more when the relaxation is done.

www.ingramcontent.com/pod-product-compliance
Lightning Source LLC
Chambersburg PA
CBHW070827100426
42813CB00003B/522